Thematic Poems, Songs and Fingerplays

45 Irresistible Rhymes and Activities To Build Literacy

by Meish Goldish

SCHOLASTIC
PROFESSIONAL BOOKS

NEW YORK • TORONTO • LONDON • AUCKLAND • SYDNEY

Cover design and art by Vincent Ceci
Interior design by Jacqueline Swensen
Interior illustration by Jan Pyk

ISBN 0-590-49638-7

TABLE OF CONTENTS

Continued

Continued

Places Near and Far

Working and Playing

Friends, Family, and Me

Welcome to *Thematic Poems, Songs, and Fingerplays!* Integrating these irresistible verses into your curriculum will delight children and give them opportunities to discover the richness of language. They are also an ideal instructional tool for introducing or reinforcing thematic learning.

The reading and chanting of poems and fingerplays or the joy of a sing-a-long provide shared-reading experiences in which all children can be successful. These rich opportunities also develop the sense of being part of a community of readers and help to build important early literacy skills such as:

- ▶ understanding the concept of word;
- ▶ recognizing words by sight;
- ▶ noticing language patterns and rhymes;
- ▶ connecting sound to print; and
- ▶ learning about directionality, spacing, and other components of prints.

Thematic Poems, Songs, and Fingerplays offers many ways to empower children and foster a love of learning. Opportunities to participate in small groups or perform individually will develop a spirit of cooperation and build self-esteem. Invitations to embellish a selection by creating a prop or playing a simple musical instrument will spark creativity. And more good news: These poems and songs offer a natural extension for creating new verses or encouraging other kinds of writing.

Each of the 45 poems and songs in this book includes a special page filled with ideas for reading the selection, extension activities, and a list of theme-related children's books.

The verses themselves can be presented in a number of ways. For example, you might copy them onto large chart paper, prepare transparencies for the overhead projector, or provide students with individual photocopies—it's up to you and the needs and interests of your students. There are many ways to use *Poems, Songs, and Fingerplays*, but only one rule: Have fun!

EAT THE ALPHABET

A is Apple, B is Bean,
C is Celery, fresh and green.

D is Doughnut, E is Egg,
F is Fig, rolling down your leg!

G is Grapefruit, H is Honey,
I is Ice cream, soft and runny.

J is Jello, K is Knish,
L is Lettuce and Lic-o-rice!

M is Meatball, N is Nut,
O is Orange, peeled or cut.

P is Pizza, Q is Quince,
R is Rice fit for a prince!

S is Spaghetti, T is Tangerine,
U is Upside-down cake with cream between.

V is Vegetable soup, W is Waffle,
X is scrambled X. (Isn't that joke awful!)

Y is Yogurt, Z is Zucchini,
Let's eat the alphabet on a bed of linguine!

Suggestions for Sharing

○ Have each child write a different letter of the alphabet on a paper plate. Then have children stand shoulder to shoulder in a straight line, taking turns stepping forward and displaying their letters while reciting the corresponding lines from the poem. Or have children use their fingers to write each letter in the air as it is mentioned in the poem.

○ Let each child find or draw a picture of the food that matches his or her letter. As they recite individual lines from the poem, children can display their foods along with their letters.

Thematic Activities

○ Have children choose classroom items and identify the letter of the alphabet that begins the name of each item. Tape a label with that letter on the item. For example, tape a D label on the door and a W label on the window. See how many different letters of the alphabet children can use.

○ Play a game of Human Spelling. Have children hold paper plates with the letters of the alphabet marked on them. Call out a word such as *cat*, and have the children holding the C, A, and T plates step forward and stand side by side in order to spell the word.

Classroom Resources

○ *Anno's Alphabet* by Mitsumasa Anno, Crowell, 1975

○ *On Market Street* by Arnold Lobel, Greenwillow, 1981

○ *Under the Sea from A to Z* by Anne Doubilet, Crown, 1991

IT ALL ADDS UP

Once there was a lonely son,
Sad 'cause he was only **one**.

Then along came Cindy Lou,
Now they were a happy **two**!

Next they met Joanne Marie,
That made them a happy **three**!

Then along came Salvador,
Now they were a happy **four**!

Soon they saw Roberto Clive,
That made them a happy **five**!

They went to the house of Nick's,
Where they were a happy **six**!

Then along came Kenneth Kevin,
That made them a happy **seven**!

Next they met Melissa Kate,
Now they were a happy **eight**!

Then along came Caroline,
That made them a happy **nine**!

Finally they all met Gwen,
Ending up a happy **ten**!

Suggestions for Sharing

○ Have children hold up their fingers to indicate the number mentioned at the end of every other line. Tell them to place a special emphasis on each number as they recite it.

○ Assign a role to each child (e.g., the lonely son, Cindy Lou, Joanne Marie). As each character is mentioned, have that child join the previous characters in line, so by the end of the poem all ten children are lined up.

Thematic Activities

○ Have children stand in line and practice counting off. The first child calls "One!" and succeeding children call out their numbers. Then rearrange the line and have children count off again. Challenge the group to see how quickly they can count off each time.

○ Invite children to make up simple addition problems for their classmates to solve. For example: If two people get in a car, and then three more people join them, how many people are there in all? Let children use manipulatives such as buttons or paper clips to demonstrate the answer.

Classroom Resources

○ *Anno's Counting Book* by Mitsumasa Anno, Crowell, 1977

○ *One Hungry Monster* by Susan Heyboer O'Keefe, Joy Street, 1989

○ *Up to Ten and Down Again* by Lisa Campbell, Ernst, Lothrop, Lee, & Shepard, 1986

I LOVE COLORS

CHORUS:
I love colors, yes I do!
Red and orange and green and blue!
I love colors, dark or bright,
Yellow, purple, black, and white!

What is red? Juicy beets!
What is brown? Chocolate treats!
What is white? A shiny moon!
What is gray? A big baboon!

CHORUS

What is orange? Carrot sticks!
What is yellow? Baby chicks!
What is gold? Bright goldfish!
What is black? Licorice!

CHORUS

What is green? Grass so high!
What is blue? The open sky!
What is purple? Eggplant shells!
What is silver? Silver bells!

CHORUS

Suggestions for Sharing

○ Divide the class into two groups. Have both groups recite the chorus together. For the verses, have one group ask the questions (e.g., "What is red?") and the other group give the responses (e.g., "Juicy beets!").

○ Have the children hold up sheets of construction paper of different colors. Let them display their individual colors as they recite the chorus and verses of the poem. You may also have children display pictures of the items mentioned throughout the poem.

Thematic Activities

○ Divide the class into groups, assigning each a different color. Have members of each group search through magazines to find items of that color. Let them create a collage from their collection.

○ Let children conduct experiments to see what results from mixing two different colors of paints or crayons. For example, children will discover that red and yellow yield orange, yellow and blue yield green, and blue and red yield purple.

Classroom Resources

○ *Color Zoo* by Lois Ehlert, Lippincott, 1989

○ *Freight Train* by Donald Crews, Puffin, 1985

○ *My Very First Book of Colors* by Eric Carle, Crowell, 1974

THE SHAPE OF THINGS

What is a circle? What is round?
A quarter rolling on the ground.
A wheel is a circle, so is the moon,
A bottle cap, or a big balloon.

What is a square, with sides the same?
The wooden board for a checker game.
A slice of cheese, a TV screen,
A table napkin to keep you clean.

What is a rectangle, straight and tall?
The door that stands within your wall.
A dollar bill, a loaf of bread,
The mattress lying on your bed.

What is a triangle, with sides of three?
A piece of pie for you and me.
A musical triangle, ding, ding, ding,
A slice of pizza with everything!

These are the shapes seen everywhere:
A triangle, rectangle, circle, square.
If you look closely where you've been,
You'll surely see the shapes you're in!

Suggestions for Sharing

○ Have children use their thumbs and index fingers to form each of the four shapes as they recite the poem. Or have them use their index fingers alone to draw each shape in the air as they recite.

○ Children may bring to class some of the items mentioned in the poem. As they recite, have them hold up each item at the appropriate time.

Thematic Activities

○ Divide the class into four groups, assigning each a different shape. Have them go on a Shape Hunt to search for classroom items that have their assigned shape. Later, let each group display the items they found.

○ Play a variation on Concentration by preparing eight or more index cards, each bearing a circle, square, rectangle, or triangle (each card should have a match). Lay the cards face down. Players take turns turning two cards over in an attempt to make a match. A player keeps the cards if they have the same shape and the player can correctly name it.

Classroom Resources

○ *Pancakes, Crackers, and Pizza: A Book of Shapes* by Marjorie Eberts and Margaret Gisler, Childrens Press, 1984

○ *Shapes and Colors* by Denise Lewis Patrick, Western, 1990

○ *Shapes, Shapes, Shapes* by Tana Hoban, Greenwillow, 1986

DAYS OF THE WEEK

(sung to "Sing a Song of Sixpence")

Sing a song of Monday,
Helping to shop.
Sing a song of Tuesday,
Popcorn to pop.
Sing a song of Wednesday,
Books to begin.
Sing a song of Thursday,
When I play the violin!

Sing a song of Friday,
Riding my bike.
Sing a song of Saturday,
Taking a hike.
Sing a song of Sunday,
Out playing ball.
Every day of every week's
My favorite day of all!

Suggestions for Sharing

○ Have children line up, each holding a sign that names a day of the week. As each day is sung about, children with that sign step forward and display it.

○ Encourage children to perform the actions of the song as they sing. For example, they can pretend to be pushing a shopping cart, popping popcorn, reading a book, playing the violin, and so on.

Thematic Activities

○ Provide students with copies of journal sheets complete with sentence starters designed to help them describe the activities that take place at various times in their day. The sentence starters might read as follows:

○ When I wake up I...

○ Before lunch I...

○ After lunch I...

○ Before dinner I...

○ After dinner I...

○ Before bedtime I...

Allow time for students to share their entries. Consider having students refer to completed journals to create charts titled "Each Day We Do Some of the Same Things" and "Each Day We Do Some Things Differently." On the first chart, list items that all (or most) of the students have in common. On the second chart, list items that were mentioned only once by individual students. If desired, entries may also note particular days of the week events occur ("On Tuesday we go to gym," or, "On Saturday David goes to swimming lessons.")

Classroom Resources

○ *Cookie's Week* by Cindy Ward, Putnam, 1988

○ *One Monday Morning* by Uri Shulevitz, Aladdin, 1986

○ *Today Is Monday* by Harriet Ziefert, HarperCollins, 1992

MONTHS AND SEASONS

January, February, middle of March,
Brrr! In the cold I'm stiff as starch!
Let's make a snowball, sled down a hill.
Wintertime, wintertime, time to chill!

April, May, to the middle of June,
Ahh! What a nice, cool afternoon!
Let's fly a kite, and plant pretty flowers.
Springtime, springtime, time for showers!

July and August, middle of September,
Ouch! Got a sunburn I'll always remember!
Let's go swimming, let's eat a peach.
Summertime, summertime, time for the beach!

October, November, middle of December,
Hey! Each day grows shorter than September!
Let's see the leaves fall, let's bake a cake.
Autumntime, autumntime, time for a rake!

Hooray for the seasons all through the year,
One just left and another one's here!
I love the seasons, each is a ball:
Wintertime, springtime, summertime, fall!

Suggestions for Sharing

○ After reviewing the seasonal symbols noted in the poem, divide students into four groups. Have each group choose one of the four seasons. Then have students in each group work together to think of additional symbols representing their season. Ask students to draw or paint their seasonal symbols on manila paper which has been trimmed to represent a banner. Then have each group choose one representative to hold its seasonal banner. Show the four banner-holders how to stand back-to-back to form a tight circle. As you read the poem, have the students turn themselves so that the correct seasonal banner is facing the class. (For this activity to work, banners must be arranged in seasonal order. You may want students to discover this for themselves.)

○ Invite children to act out the actions of the poem as they recite. For example, for the verse about winter, some children might stand stiffly as if freezing, others may pantomime the packing of a snowball, and others may pretend to be sledding down a hill.

Thematic Activities

○ Encourage children to describe what they like most about each of the four seasons of the year. Have them discuss their favorite activities and holidays for each season. Then have groups of children create a large calendar page for each month of the year, filling it in with information such as classmates' birthdays, seasonal holidays, and other special events. Post the calendar on the bulletin board to serve as a year-long reference.

○ Organize four groups of children and have each group prepare a large collage of magazine pictures depicting activities appropriate for a particular season. Each group should provide a heading for their collage, such as "We Love Springtime!" Display all collages on the classroom wall.

Classroom Resources

○ *Chicken Soup with Rice* by Maurice Sendak, HarperCollins, 1962

○ *January Brings the Snow: A Book of Months* by Jenni Oliver, Dial, 1986

○ *Seasons on the Farm* by Jane Miller, J. M. Dent & Sons, 1986

THE FOOD TO EAT

(sung to "Do You Know the Muffin Man?")

CHORUS:
Do you know the food to eat,
The food to eat, the food to eat?
Do you know the food to eat
To make you big and strong?

Muffins, bagels, toast, and bread,
Eat your cereal, get ahead!
Noodles, pizzas, what a spread
To make you big and strong!

CHORUS

Apples, oranges, corn, and beets,
Carrots, lettuce, juicy treats!
Fruits and veggies are the eats
To make you big and strong!

CHORUS

Beef and chicken, eggs, and fish,
Nuts and beans are so delish!
Meat can be a tasty dish
To make you big and strong!

CHORUS

Milk and yogurt, low-fat cheese,
Just a little ice cream please.
Dairy foods are foods like these
To make you big and strong!

CHORUS

Suggestions for Sharing

○ After acquainting students with the particulars of the food pyramid, offer them a blank food pyramid cut from solid-colored felt. Have students cut magazine pictures of food corresponding to each segment of the pyramid. Then use two-sided tape to adhere the pictures to the felt. As you read the poem, have students take turns assembling the pyramid on a flannel board.

○ Have children bring to class either the actual foods mentioned in the poem, empty food containers, or pictures of the foods. Divide the class into four groups. Let each group recite one of the verses while displaying the foods that belong in their group.

Thematic Activities

○ Hold a pretend Taste Test in the classroom. Have each student think of a favorite food and then jot down words describing the look, taste, texture and smell of that food. (Remind children to think of words appealing to the five senses.) Then have each student take turns describing his or her favorite food as the class pretends to chew and swallow. For example, a student describing potato chips might say, "You are eating a flat, round, crunchy snack. It is salty and a little oily. It smells like potatoes." (You might want to model describing a few of your favorite foods before asking students to describe their own.)

○ Have children each draw a picture of their favorite breakfast, lunch, or dinner. Let individuals display their pictures, identify each food, and tell classmates to which food group each food belongs.

Classroom Resources

○ *My Very First Book of Food* by Eric Carle, Crowell, 1986

○ *What's on My Plate?* by Ruth Belov Gross, Macmillan, 1990

○ *What's on Your Plate?* by Norah Smaridge, Abingdon, 1982

THE FIVE SENSES

Use your senses, what do they tell?
Look, sound, taste, feel, and smell!
Use your senses, show you're alive,
Use your senses, use all five!

Use your eyes to see what's there.
Is it round or is it square?
What's its color? What's its size?
Use your senses, use your eyes!

Use your hands to feel a lot.
Is it cold or is it hot?
Is it squishy like rubber bands?
Use your senses, use your hands!

Use your ears to hear the noise.
Does it rattle or squeak like toys?
Is it quiet, or loud as cheers?
Use your senses, use your ears!

Use your tongue to learn the taste.
Is it sweet as mint toothpaste?
Does it tingle like a bee that has stung?
Use your senses, use your tongue!

Use your nose to smell what's there.
Is something fishy in the air?
Is it fresh as a daisy or rose?
Use your senses, use your nose!

Suggestions for Sharing

○ As children recite the poem, have them point to their eyes, hands, ears, tongue, and nose at the appropriate time. Also have them act out details in the poem, such as forming a circle and square with their fingers or pretending to touch something hot or cold.

○ Divide the class into five groups. After all groups recite the first verse of the poem together, have individual groups recite each of the remaining five verses. Each group may hold up a large picture of the part of the body it represents.

Thematic Activities

○ Place a mystery item into a shoe box. Without opening the box, have students guess what's inside. Repeat the game with other items until everyone has had a chance to participate. Also try repeating the activity using a paper bag to conceal objects. Ask the children to tell if the type of container does or does not make a difference when trying to guess contents.

○ In a variation on the game above, have each child think of an item and describe it for classmates without naming it. The description may tell how it looks, feels, tastes, smells, or sounds. See how many classmates can correctly guess the item from the description.

Classroom Resources

○ *The Five Senses* by Keith Brandt, Troll, 1985

○ *How Does It Feel? Exploring the World of Your Senses* by Mick Csaky, Harmony Books, 1979

○ *Is It Rough? Is It Smooth? Is It Shiny?* by Tana Hoban, Greenwillow, 1984

GREEN PLANTS

(sung to "Three Blind Mice")

Three main things, three main things,
Green plants need, green plants need.
For plants to grow, for plants to thrive,
In order to keep green plants alive,
What does it take so they'll survive?
Three main things!

Plants need sun, plants need sun,
That's number one, plants need sun.
For plants to grow, for plants to thrive,
In order to keep green plants alive,
What does it take so they'll survive?
Plants need sun!

Plants need air, plants need air,
Be aware, plants need air.
For plants to grow, for plants to thrive,
In order to keep green plants alive,
What does it take so they'll survive?
Plants need air!

Plants need water, plants need water,
'Specially when it's hotter, plants need water.
For plants to grow, for plants to thrive,
In order to keep green plants alive,
What does it take so they'll survive?
Plants need water!

Suggestions for Sharing

○ Have children hold up one, two, and three fingers as they sing about the first, second, and third needs of green plants. They may also form their arms in a large circle to represent the sun, wave their hands about to represent air, and wiggle their fingers in a downward motion to represent water.

○ Organize children into three groups. After everyone sings the first verse together, have each group sing a subsequent verse. While singing, children may first crouch down and then slowly rise, to suggest a growing plant.

Thematic Activities

○ To demonstrate the three needs of green plants, take two green plants. Leave one where it will get no water, no sunlight, and little air. Give the other plant all three elements. Let children observe the plants daily and describe how they begin to differ in appearance over time.

○ To demonstrate how green plants take in water through their roots and into their leaves, add red food coloring to a glass of water. Place a fresh stalk of celery with leaves attached in the colored water. After a few hours, have children note how the coloring has made its way to the celery leaves.

Classroom Resources

○ *How Do Plants Get Food?* by Meish Goldish, Raintree, 1989

○ *Play With Plants* by Millicent Selsam, Morrow, 1978

○ *Seeds: Pop! Stick! Glide!* by Patricia Lauber, Crown, 1988

IF I HAD A PET

CHORUS:
If I had a pet, pet, pet,
Which one would I get, get, get?
If I had a pet, pet, pet
To care for and to play with.

For a puppy of my own,
I would find a juicy bone.
Walk my puppy every day,
Teach it how to fetch and stay!

CHORUS

For a kitten I would bring
A playful little ball of string.
Pour some milk into a cup,
Watch my kitty lap it up!

CHORUS

For a fish I'd have a tank,
Making sure it ate and drank.
Feed it daily once or twice,
Change the water, keep it nice!

CHORUS

For a bird I'd bring some seed,
And a cage the bird would need.
Listen as it chirped its song,
Sing out, birdie, all day long!

CHORUS

Suggestions for Sharing

○ Pair students off, with one student partner representing a pet and the other student partner representing the pet owner. As you recite the poem, have the pets and the owners act out their respective parts. Have partners switch roles and repeat the activity.

○ Encourage children to draw or find pictures of dogs, cats, fish, and birds in magazines. As each verse is read, children with that type of animal can hold it up for all to see.

Thematic Activities

○ Take a survey in class to determine what the children's favorite pets are. Display the results in a bar graph which may then be used for a math exercise. (Ask, for example, "How many more children like dogs than birds?")

○ Invite children to bring their pets to class and talk about how they care for them. Children who cannot bring their actual pets may display photos instead. Encourage audience members to ask questions after each presentation.

Classroom Resources

○ *The Big Book of Pets* by Margaret Green, Watts, 1966

○ *Pet Mania* by Ed Radlauer, Childrens Press, 1980

○ *Pets* by Dave King, Aladdin, 1991

BUGS

June bug, stinkbug,
Ladybug, chinch bug,
Water bug, pink bug,
Please-don't-pinch bug!

Horsefly, housefly,
Dragonfly, deer fly,
Firefly, fruit fly,
Buzzing-in-your-ear fly!

Honeybee, bumblebee,
Queen bee, drone bee,
Worker bee, nurse bee,
Leave-me-alone bee!

Gypsy moth, luna moth,
Beetle and mosquito.
Bugs and insects
Really are neat-o!

Cockroach, katydid,
Cricket and cicada,
Grasshopper, mantid,
Catch you all later!

Suggestions for Sharing

○ To emphasize the steady rhythm of this poem, have children snap their fingers or clap their hands softly as they recite each verse. They may gradually increase their volume as the recital progresses.

○ Divide the class into five groups. Assign each group a different verse of the poem to recite. Children may wiggle their fingers to imitate the movements of the bugs and insects as they recite their lines.

Thematic Activities

○ Ask children if they can name other bugs and insects besides those in the poem. (They might mention termites, ants, butterflies, walking sticks, and fleas, for example.) Let volunteers tell how they know about each kind of insect and describe its features.

○ Have children each choose a different bug or insect to learn more about. Let them prepare information cards on their creatures. One side of the card should have a drawing of the bug or insect, and the other side should contain a few interesting facts such as its size, color, home, food, etc. Put the cards in your insect learning center for students to explore.

Classroom Resources

○ *A Big Book of Bugs* by Haris Petie, Prentice-Hall, 1977

○ *Bugs for Dinner?* by Sam and Beryl Epstein, Macmillan, 1989

○ *You Can Make an Insect Zoo* by Hortense Roberts, Childrens Press, 1974

LIFE OF A BUTTERFLY

(sung to "The Eensy Weensy Spider")

A butterfly begins
By laying all her eggs.
Out pops a caterpillar
Crawling on its legs.
The caterpillar first is
Very, very thin,
But it eats and eats and eats
Till it bursts out through its skin!

Soon the caterpillar's
Grown nice and big.
So it climbs on top
Of a tiny leaf or twig.
It makes a hard shell
And there it hangs inside.
The shell soon cracks
And then the parts divide.

Now here's a fact
That's really, really strange:
Inside the shell
There's been a major change!
When the shell opens,
What comes out?
A beautiful butterfly
Fluttering about!

28

Suggestions for Sharing

○ Have children use their fingers to imitate the movements of the caterpillar in the song. For example, they may wiggle one finger to show the caterpillar crawling, and open their hand wide to show the caterpillar "bursting" through its skin.

○ Have children use cupped hands to represent the caterpillar's hard shell. Have them open their hands to show how the shell divides, and flap their hands to show the butterfly flying away.

Thematic Activities

○ Use a science book to show students pictures of a butterfly at different stages of its development. Organize children into four groups. Then offer each group a large sheet of oaktag on which you've printed one stanza or portion of a stanza of "Life of a Butterfly." (Hint: Divide the first stanza of the poem into two parts, with one part representing the butterfly laying eggs and the other part representing the caterpillar popping out of the egg.) Invite groups to paint or draw their assigned stage of development. When all illustrations are complete, place pages together between two additional pieces of oaktag. Punch three holes down the left-hand side of the sheets and use ribbon or looseleaf rings to bind pages together into a big book. On the cover of the book, create overlapping butterfly shapes by tracing around pairs of students' feet with different colored crayons. Print students' names on their butterfly wings.

○ Ask children to describe different kinds of butterflies they have seen. Have each child draw a large picture of a beautiful butterfly and then cut it out. Fold the wings to make the butterfly look like it is flying. Pin all artwork on the bulletin board.

Classroom Resources

○ *The Caterpillar and the Polliwog* by Jack Kent, Prentice-Hall, 1982

○ *The Very Hungry Caterpillar* by Eric Carle, Philomel, 1979

○ *Where Butterflies Grow* by Joanne Ryder, Lodestar, 1989

LITTLE BROWN BEAR

(sung to "Little Brown Jug")

CHORUS:
Ha ha ha, hee hee hee,
Little brown bear, where can you be?
Ha ha ha, hee hee hee,
Little brown bear, where can you be?

In the woods, in your den?
Are you off to hunt again?
Use your teeth, use your claws,
Catch a fish between your paws!

CHORUS

Furry coat, nice and thick,
Legs and feet that really kick!
You'll grow big, you'll grow strong,
You'll grow up to nine feet long!

CHORUS

In the zoo, in a cave,
How I hope that you'll behave!
In a log, in your lair,
Will you be my teddy bear?

CHORUS

Suggestions for Sharing

○ Have children place their hands over their eyes, as if looking for the bear, while singing "Where can you be?" Also have them act out the motions of catching a fish with their paws and kicking with their feet.

○ Help students turn the song into a rebus display. Begin by printing the lyrics on a large piece of chart-pad paper. Then help students choose those lyrics that they may want to illustrate ("Little brown bear... the woods... furry coat...," etc.). Provide students with removable sticky notes which may be used to cover selected words on the chart. Students can then illustrate the words on the sticky notes, place the notes over the corresponding words, and refer to the rebus chart when singing or reciting the song. Students may also lift the notes to read the words underneath.

Thematic Activities

○ Invite children to bring toy bears to class. Have them retell the story of "The Three Bears" or make up their own story to act out, using their stuffed animals as characters.

○ Hold a "Teddy Bear Picnic" in your classroom. Serve popular bear foods such as honey, nuts, fruits, and jam. Have children pretend to be bears as they hold a growling contest.

Classroom Resources

○ *Ask Mr. Bear* by Marjorie Flack, Macmillan, 1986

○ *Bears* by Ruth Krauss, Scholastic, 1968

○ *Brown Bear, Brown Bear, What Do You See?* by Bill Martin, Jr., Holt, 1983

TIME FOR HIBERNATION

(sung to "Frere Jacques")

Are you sleeping, are you sleeping,
Big brown bear, big brown bear?
Time for hibernation. What is your location?
In a log, in a lair.

Are you sleeping, are you sleeping,
Little frog, little frog?
Time for hibernation. What is your location?
In a pond, near a log.

Are you sleeping, are you sleeping,
Hanging bat, hanging bat?
Time for hibernation. What is your location?
In a cave is where I'm at.

Are you sleeping, are you sleeping,
Slinky snake, slinky snake?
Time for hibernation. What is your location?
In the mud, in a lake.

Are you sleeping, are you sleeping,
Turtle friend, turtle friend?
Time for hibernation. What is your location?
In the stream, till winter's end!

Suggestions for Sharing

○ Assign some children to be the animals in the song, and other children to be the chorus. The chorus sings the first three lines of each verse, leaning their heads on their hands to indicate sleeping. Then have the animals respond by singing the last line of each verse.

○ Have children use socks to create instant puppets corresponding to the animals featured in the song. Students may use a brown sock to represent the bear, a grey sock to represent the snake, green socks to represent the frog and the turtle, and a black sock to represent the bat. Cut extra body parts (eyes, legs, wings, shell, etc.) from construction paper and tape to the sock bases. Students can then take turns using the puppets to sing the song.

Thematic Activities

○ Let children create a mural that shows the homes in which various kinds of animals hibernate. On long sheets of butcher paper, children may draw pictures of caves, logs, ponds, streams, and other places where animals rest for the winter. Then have the children find magazine pictures of the animals and paste them into their proper homes.

○ Help children learn more facts about animals and their hibernation habits. Then have students record and illustrate their findings in a hibernation book. First invite students to draw hibernating animals on manila paper and then show students how to conceal the animals with sticky notes decorated to resemble hibernation hiding spots.

Classroom Resources

○ *Animals in Winter* by Henrietta Bancroft and Richard Van Gelder, Crowell, 1963

○ *Animals That Hibernate* by Larry Dane Brimner, Watts, 1991

○ *Why Do Animals Sleep Through the Winter?* by Chris Arvetis, Childrens Press, 1987

ANIMALS IN DANGER!

CHORUS:
Danger! Danger!
Animals in danger!
Animals in danger
May not survive.
Help them! Help them!
We want to help them!
We want to help them
Stay alive!

The Bengal tiger,
The mountain gorilla,
The African elephant,
The whooping crane.
The California condor,
The Asian rhinoceros,
We want to help them
All remain!

CHORUS

What can we do
For animals in danger?
What can we do
So they'll survive?
Never, ever hunt them,
Never take their homes away.
That is the way
They'll stay alive!

Suggestions for Sharing

○ Help children locate pictures of each animal mentioned in the poem. (Encyclopedias, children's nature magazines, and nonfiction books on endangered species are all good sources for animal pictures.) Invite children to draw pictures of the animals on cards, which they can hold up as they recite the poem.

○ Have children cover their faces with their hands, as if in distress, during the first four lines of the chorus. Then have them hold their hands out, as if offering help, during the last four lines.

Thematic Activities

○ Talk about the reasons why animals become extinct (hunting, loss of habitats, difficulty mating in foreign environments, pollution, etc.). Have children brainstorm ways they can help protect animals. Record all ideas. Also, write a class letter to a wildlife conservation group requesting additional ideas students may implement, and add these to your list. Decide together on one idea to pursue as a group (reducing trash, conserving water, collecting money to donate to a preserve, etc.) Decide also on a way to keep track of your efforts.

○ Have children imagine what two or more endangered animals might say to one another if they could talk. Let children work with partners to create a conversation and perform it for classmates.

Classroom Resources

○ *Endangered Animal* by Malcolm Penny, Bookwright Press, 1988

○ *Endangered Animals* by Lynn Stone, Childrens Press, 1984

○ *Animals in Danger* by Marcus Schneck, Gallery, 1990

GIANT DINOSAURS

Giant dinosaurs roaming around,
Stomping their feet and shaking the ground!

Hungry dinosaurs eating their lunch,
Chewing on a treetop—crunch! crunch! crunch!

Angry dinosaurs having a fight,
Kicking and biting with all their might!

Baby dinosaurs hatching from eggs,
Growing sharp teeth and leathery legs!

Playful dinosaurs finding it fun,
Dipping in the lake in the afternoon sun!

Thick-skinned dinosaurs wearing hard scales,
Snapping their heads and giant tails!

Tired-out dinosaurs falling asleep,
Lying on a grass bed, oh so deep!

So many dinosaurs living long ago.
Why did they disappear? No one seems to know!

Suggestions for Sharing

○ Pair off the children, and have each pair act out the motions of the dinosaurs in one of the verses. For example, the first pair of children might walk with their feet stomping heavily.

○ Ask children to bring their toy dinosaurs into school. Then decide which of the toy dinosaurs would best represent each of the types described in the poem ("Giant dinosaurs...hungry dinosaurs...angry dinosaurs," etc.). Arrange chairs side by side in a row. Have students sit on the chairs and take turns holding and manipulating each type of dinosaur as the lines of the poem are recited.

Thematic Activities

○ Help children learn more about the many kinds of dinosaurs that once existed. Have them each choose their favorite type of dinosaur and make a Dinosaur Card for it. On one side of a card, have them draw a picture of their dinosaur. On the other side, have them list interesting information such as the creature's size and eating habits. Display all cards in a dinosaur learning center for students to explore.

○ Explain that no one knows for sure why the dinosaurs died out. Have children learn about the different theories that scientists have proposed. Then let them each decide which theory they agree with and explain why.

Classroom Resources

○ *Dinosaur Bones* by Aliki, Crowell, 1988

○ *Dinosaurs* by Gail Gibbons, Holiday House, 1987

○ *Giant Dinosaurs* by Erna Rowe, Scholastic, 1973

GEORGE WASHINGTON

CHORUS:
George, George Washington,
You're, you're number one!
George, George Washington,
You're number one to me!

Leader of the army,
An able general, George.
Strongly and bravely,
You led at Valley Forge!

CHORUS

Father of our country,
Our first President.
Proudly and wisely,
You led the government!

CHORUS

We celebrate your birthday,
Our capital has your name.
Your picture's on a dollar bill,
So all will know your fame!

CHORUS

You never told a lie, George,
You were brave and smart.
First in honor, first in peace,
First in our heart!

CHORUS

Suggestions for Sharing

○ Each time children recite the chorus, have them hold up their index fingers to indicate "number one." For the verses, have them act out movements to suggest the details that are mentioned. For example, they may march in place to indicate leading the army.

○ Have children create tri-cornered hats reminiscent of George Washington's by stapling the ends of three 4-1/2 by 12 inch strips of black construction paper together to fit their heads. Have students parade around wearing the hats as they recite the poem. You might also play selections of patriotic parade music for students to march to.

Thematic Activities

○ Ask children to imagine they were news reporters at the time of George Washington. Have them prepare a newscast about his victory in the Revolutionary War or his becoming our first President. Invite them to "broadcast" their reports to the class.

○ Have children design a new postage stamp to commemorate the life of George Washington. Let volunteers display their work and describe the scenes they have drawn.

Classroom Resources

○ *George Washington* by Laurence Santrey, Troll, 1982

○ *George Washington* by Brian Williams, Cavendish, 1988

○ *A Picture Book of George Washington* by David Adler, Holiday House, 1989

PRESIDENT LINCOLN

(sung to "Reuben, Reuben, I've Been Thinkin'")

President Lincoln, I've been thinkin'
When you were a tiny babe.
As a youth, you told the truth,
So people called you "Honest Abe."

President Lincoln, I've been thinkin'
You grew up as tough as nails.
On the farm, you swung your arm,
And with an axe you split the rails!

President Lincoln, I've been thinkin'
How you taught yourself the law.
Every book around you took,
And read like no one ever saw!

President Lincoln, I've been thinkin'
Back to when you wrote the E-
Mancipation Proclamation,
So the slaves could all be free.

President Lincoln, I've been thinkin'
How you bravely led the land.
Once divided, now united,
You made sure our house would stand!

Suggestions for Sharing

○ Have children perform Lincoln's actions as they sing the song. They may pretend to be swinging an axe, reading a book, and writing the Emancipation Proclamation.

○ Children may recite the song in Abraham Lincoln costumes. Stovepipe hats can be made from cardboard rolled into a tube and stapled at the sides. Children may also wear beards cut from black construction paper.

Thematic Activities

○ Help children learn more about the important events in Abraham Lincoln's life. On a long sheet of butcher paper, create a time line that indicates the year of each significant event.

○ Have children pair off to conduct an interview with Abraham Lincoln. One partner should be the interviewer and the other should be Lincoln, who answers questions about his life or offers opinions on issues of our own times. When ready, partners may perform their interviews for the class.

Classroom Resources

○ *Abe Lincoln, the Young Years* by Keith Brandt, Troll, 1982

○ *Honest Abe* by Edith Kunhardt, Greenwillow, 1993

○ *A Picture Book of Abraham Lincoln* by David Adler, Holiday House, 1989

DR. MARTIN LUTHER KING, JR.

CHORUS:
"I have a dream!"
"I have a dream!"
These were the words
Of Martin Luther King.
What was his dream?
What was his dream?
Tell us the dream
Of Martin Luther King.

Dr. King wished,
Dr. King prayed
That one day all people
Would live unafraid.
Dr. King cared
For blacks and for whites.
He wanted all people
To share equal rights.

CHORUS

Dr. King marched,
Dr. King spoke
Of a world full of justice
For all kinds of folk.
Dr. King cared
For me and for you.
By working together,
His dream can come true!

CHORUS

Suggestions for Sharing

○ Help children find pictures of Dr. Martin Luther King, Jr. in books and magazines. As they sing the song, have them take turns holding up their pictures.

○ Divide students into thirds. Give each group an opportunity to recite the chorus once during the reading.

Thematic Activities

○ Have children plan ways to celebrate Martin Luther King Day in class. For example, they might sing songs about freedom, listen to recordings of King's speeches, or write their own poems about King.

○ Have children paint a giant mural with pictures and symbols representing the work of Dr. Martin Luther King, Jr. Later, let children point out the individual details in the mural and explain their significance.

Classroom Resources

○ *If You Lived at the Time of Martin Luther King* by Ellen Levine, Scholastic, 1990

○ *Martin Luther King* by Rae Bains, Troll, 1984

○ *Martin Luther King Day* by Linda Lowery, Carolrhoda Books, 1987

CHRISTOPHER COLUMBUS

Christopher Columbus was one of a kind.
A way to the Indies he wanted to find.
People said, "Chris, you'll never succeed."
But he had a plan, he had a need.

Sailing from Spain was Chris's idea,
On the Nina, the Pinta, and the Santa Maria.
People said, "Chris, you'll fall off the earth."
But he followed his dream for all it was worth.

The year was 1492
When Columbus set off with an eager crew.
People said, "Chris, you'll never reach land."
But on he sailed, just as planned.

Two months later, an island was found.
There were Native Americans all around.
Chris and his crew began to explore
What the Indians discovered long before.

Chris didn't know the trip he led
Was not to the Indies, but America instead!
Even so, he gained such fame
That now the whole world knows his name!

Suggestions for Sharing

○ Have children use their fingers to act out the different parts of the poem. For example, they may hold up one finger to show "one of a kind," or form circles with their thumbs and index fingers as if looking through a telescope for the land Columbus "wanted to find."

○ Divide the children into two groups. For each verse of the poem, let the first group recite the first two lines and the second group recite the last two lines.

Thematic Activities

○ Help children learn more about the route Columbus followed to reach America. Have them trace his original route from Palos, Spain to San Salvador on a large map of the world or on a globe. Introduce or review the concepts of north, south, east, and west. Have students decide which direction Columbus traveled to reach the New World. Then, locate north, south, east, and west on a local map and have children discover which direction(s) they each must travel to get to school or other locations in the community.

○ Pair off children. Have one partner pretend to be Columbus, and the other pretend to be either a crew member during the voyage or a Native American whom Chris meets. Have them imagine a conversation the two individuals might have. Invite volunteers to perform their conversations for the class.

Classroom Resources

○ *Christopher Columbus: A Great Explorer* by Carol Greene, Childrens Press, 1989

○ *In 1492* by Jean Marzollo, Scholastic, 1991

○ *A Picture Book of Christopher Columbus* by David Adler, Holiday House, 1991

NATIVE AMERICANS

CHORUS:
Keepers of the Earth!
Keepers of the Earth!
Native Americans are
Keepers of the Earth!

Respecting the land
And all its means,
Planting corn
And squash and beans.
Respecting the land
That nature's graced,
Using it wisely,
Avoiding waste!

CHORUS

Respecting waters
Far and near,
Keeping the waters
Clean and clear.
Respecting animals
Where they roam,
Respecting land,
Respecting home!

CHORUS

Suggestions for Sharing

○ Have children spread their arms out wide each time the poem mentions "the Earth" or "the land." Also, have them act out the motions of planting food and paddling oars in the water.

○ After showing children pictures of Native Americans dressed in traditional costumes, have students pantomime getting dressed in such clothing. You might prompt children by offering directions such as, "You are now placing your feathered headdress on your head" and, "You are now putting on your deerskin moccasins." After children are "dressed," they may beat softly on small drums or use other rhythm instruments as they recite the poem.

Thematic Activities

○ Have children talk about the ways people today can show respect for our land, water, and air. Let them design posters promoting respect for nature in some way, working independently or in groups.

○ Remind children that, long ago, Native Americans developed sign language to communicate with one another. Let children work with partners to create several signs meaning things such as "Good morning," "Let's be friends," or "Thank you." Later, have them demonstrate their sign language to the whole class.

Classroom Resources

○ *Before Columbus* by Muriel Batherman, Houghton Mifflin, 1981

○ *First Came the Indians* by M. J. Wheeler, Atheneum, 1983

○ *Indians* by Teri Martini, Childrens Press, 1982

THANKSGIVING DAY

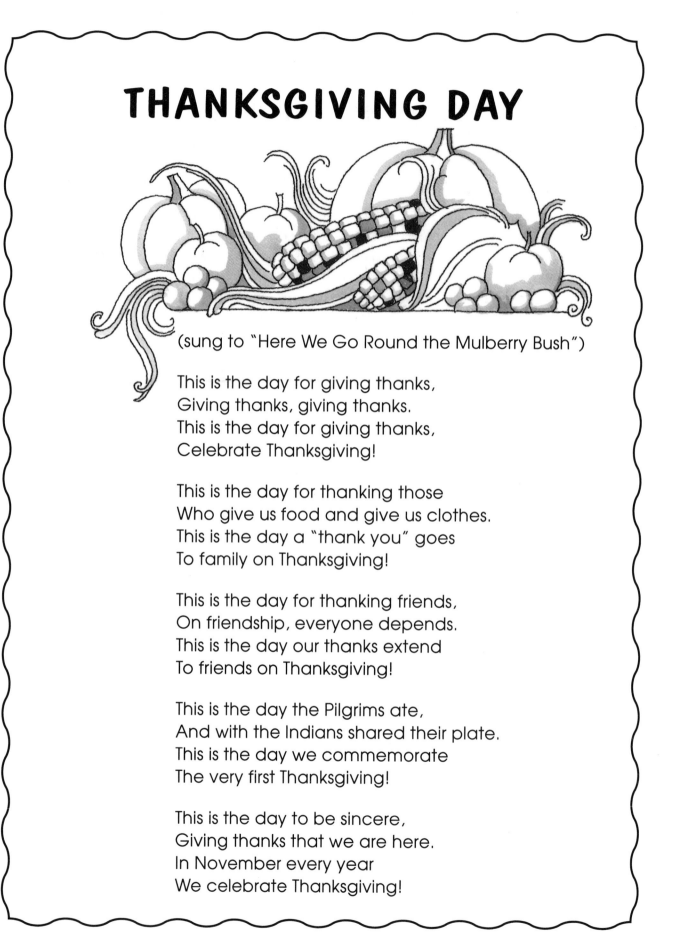

(sung to "Here We Go Round the Mulberry Bush")

This is the day for giving thanks,
Giving thanks, giving thanks.
This is the day for giving thanks,
Celebrate Thanksgiving!

This is the day for thanking those
Who give us food and give us clothes.
This is the day a "thank you" goes
To family on Thanksgiving!

This is the day for thanking friends,
On friendship, everyone depends.
This is the day our thanks extend
To friends on Thanksgiving!

This is the day the Pilgrims ate,
And with the Indians shared their plate.
This is the day we commemorate
The very first Thanksgiving!

This is the day to be sincere,
Giving thanks that we are here.
In November every year
We celebrate Thanksgiving!

Suggestions for Sharing

○ Have children cup their hands, palms up, each time they sing of "giving thanks" or mention Thanksgiving. Encourage them to make up other motions to represent activities in the song, such as pretending to pass a dish when "sharing their plate."

○ Children may fashion Pilgrims' hats from cardboard and Pilgrims' collars from white napkins to wear as costumes during their recital. Children may also display pictures of turkeys as they sing.

Thematic Activities

○ Ask children to think of something they are very thankful to have. Have them write or dictate a sentence telling about it, and draw a picture to go with it. Display all work on the bulletin board.

○ Let children design special Thanksgiving cards to give to friends or family members. After coloring and decorating the cards, children should include a brief message of thanks to the addressee.

Classroom Resources

○ *Our Thanksgiving Book* by Jane Belk Moncure, Childrens Press, 1976

○ *Thanksgiving* by Margaret Baldwin, Watts, 1983

○ *Thanksgiving Day* by Gail Gibbons, Holiday House, 1983

HALLOWEEN

Halloween, Halloween,
Time for trick or treat!
Lots of goodies in my bag,
They're lots of fun to eat!

Halloween, Halloween,
Scary things to do!
Dressing up as a ghost,
Softly calling, "Boo!"

Halloween, Halloween,
Running room to room.
Look at me, I'm a witch
Flying on my broom!

Halloween, Halloween,
Frighten you a while.
Carving out a pumpkin face
With a crooked smile!

Halloween, Halloween,
Orange balloons to burst.
I can't wait till Halloween
October thirty-first!

Suggestions for Sharing

○ Have children gather the props and costumes mentioned in the poem and use them during the recital. For example, some children may dress as ghosts in white sheets and others as witches on broomsticks.

○ Organize the class into five groups. Have each group recite one verse of the poem. Remind children to read their lines with the proper feeling. For example, those calling "Boo!" should use a soft, haunting tone, while the witches calling "Look at me" might use a cackling voice.

Thematic Activities

○ Have children draw pictures of silly or scary pumpkin faces. Place masks against children's faces to determine where eye holes should be cut. After cutting eye holes for the children, have them punch holes in the sides of their paper, insert string, and use their drawings as Halloween masks.

○ Print the second stanza of the poem on a paper, leaving a blank space instead of the word *ghost*, so that the lines read as follows:

Halloween, Halloween,
Scary things to do!
Dressing up as a _____,
Softly calling, "Boo!"

Make copies of the poem and help each student fill in the blank with a costume idea. Then have each child illustrate his or her idea in the space above the poem and sign his or her name below the poem. Staple the poems into a class collaborative book titled "Our Halloween Dress-Up Ideas."

Classroom Resources

○ *Daddy Long Ears' Halloween* by Robert Kraus, Little Simon, 1990

○ *It's Halloween* by Jack Prelutsky, Scholastic, 1987

○ *Scary, Scary Halloween* by Eve Bunting, Ticknor & Fields, 1986

VALENTINE'S DAY

(sung to "Clementine")

Take some paper, take some scissors,
Cut a heart, and then design.
Write a message in the middle:
"Will you be my Valentine?"

Take a doily, add some cupids,
Paste them all into a line.
Give your doily to your best friend
As a special Valentine!

Take a juice can, pick some flowers,
Put them in with colored twine.
Give your present to a loved one,
And they'll be your Valentine.

Take some gumdrops and some lollies,
Add some mints, eight or nine.
Make a dandy box of candy
For your sweetest Valentine!

Here's a final gift to offer,
It's a very special sign:
Give your friendship to a loved one,
To a special Valentine.

Suggestions for Sharing

○ Have groups of children pantomime the actions in each verse as they sing the song. Or have each group gather the materials mentioned in their verse and then use them as props as they sing their verse aloud.

○ Have children pair off with partners. Invite each pair of children to sing two or four lines of the song together, until the entire song has been shared by everyone.

Thematic Activities

○ Provide students with precut construction-paper hearts cut from red, pink, purple, and white paper. The hearts should be cut in a variety of sizes. Then provide students with black construction paper and glue, and challenge the children to use the hearts to design a picture representing a gift they wish they could give someone they care about. For example, the hearts could be glued down to represent a pet cat, a vase full of flowers, or a heart necklace. Children may present their pictures (complete with labels explaining the design) to their special someones.

○ Ask children to describe the ways they can share friendship, as mentioned in the song's final verse. Make a large chart listing each child's suggestion. For example: *Friends can share a joke. —Amy*

Classroom Resources

○ *"Bee My Valentine!"* by Miriam Cohen, Greenwillow, 1978

○ *It's Valentine's Day* by Jack Prelutsky, Greenwillow, 1983

○ *Valentine's Day* by Gail Gibbons, Holiday House, 1986

ALL AROUND THE NEIGHBORHOOD

All around the neighborhood,
People help each other.

The driver on the bus
Helps a girl and her mother.

The girl and her mother
See the butcher for meat.

The butcher gives a letter
To the carrier down the street.

The carrier asks the barber
To trim his mustache.

The barber sweeps the hair up,
And puts out all the trash.

The trash collector stops
When a fire truck clangs its bell.

Firefighters join police,
Who make sure that all is well.

All around the neighborhood,
There's lots that people do.

All around the neighborhood,
Who helps *you* ?

Suggestions for Sharing

○ Assign every child to be a character in the poem. Children may make simple costumes to wear, such as an apron for the butcher or a badge for the police officer. They may also use simple props, such as a pair of scissors or a broom for the barber.

○ Have children stand shoulder to shoulder in a straight line as they each recite two lines of the poem aloud. Or have the class recite the whole poem together as children act out the actions of their assigned characters.

Thematic Activities

○ Photograph (or have children draw pictures of) members of your school faculty and staff. Have students interview each person to find out how each one works to help others. Then help students mount each picture onto a piece of construction paper. Alongside each picture, glue a dialogue balloon (cut from white construction paper) printed with a quotation from that person describing what he or she does on the job to help others. Bind pages together and place a cover on the book with an additional dialogue balloon reading "School Helpers Speak Out!"

○ Help the class draw a large map of the places in the area that children visit. It might include the library, school, park, grocery store, card shop, and movie theater, for example. Talk about the kinds of jobs that people have in each place shown on the map.

Classroom Resources

○ *How Do We Have Fun?* by Caroline Arnold, Watts, 1983

○ *Let's Find Out About the Community* by Valerie Pitt, Watts, 1972

○ *The Town* by Carol Watson, Hayes, 1980

CITY LIFE, COUNTRY LIFE

(sung to "Yankee Doodle")

Farmer Johnson has a home
Way out in the country.
There are fields and hills and lakes,
And apples grow on one tree.

Farmer Johnson likes her home
In the country quiet.
Through the fields she'll often roam,
And says that you should try it!

Mister Nitty has a home
In the busy city.
Streets and people all about,
And buildings tall and pretty.

Mister Nitty likes his home
Near the city's action.
Going all about the town,
It gives him satisfaction!

We can learn from Farmer Johnson
And from Mister Nitty.
Some folks like the country life,
While others like the city!

Suggestions for Sharing

○ Suggest that children listen carefully to a line-by-line recitation of the poem so they may decide on motions to help turn the poem into a finger play. For example, children may decide to wiggle their fingers upside down to indicate "roaming" through the country and the city.

○ Organize the children into two groups: the country people and the city people. Offer members of each group index cards which may be punched through with a hole puncher, strung with yarn, decorated with images of the country or the city, and worn as medallions. Let the country people sing the first two verses, the city people sing the second two verses, and both groups sing the final verse together.

Thematic Activities

○ Have children discuss how life is different in the country and in the city. Ask them to give reasons why they would rather live in the country or the city. Create a large chart to record their responses.

○ Let children cut out magazine pictures to create collages of country scenes and city scenes. Have them title the collages "What We See in the Country" and "What We See in the City."

Classroom Resources

○ *The City Mouse and the Country Mouse* by Jody Wheeler, Grosset & Dunlap, 1985

○ *Wake Up, City* by Alvin Tresselt, Lothrop, Lee, & Shepard, 1990

○ *When I Was Young in the Mountains* by Cynthia Rylant, Dutton, 1982

HOMES ALL AROUND

(sung to "Home on the Range")

Oh give me a home
With a snow-covered dome,
In an igloo that's cozy in sleet.
Or just let me stay
In a house made of clay,
An adobe is cool in the heat.

Homes, homes all around,
In the world, many homes can be found.
A palace or tent,
An apartment to rent,
In the world, there are all kinds of homes!

Now some people float
In a house on a boat,
And in tepees they live with no floor.
And some homes are built
Very high on a stilt
So the river won't rise to the door.

Homes, homes all around,
In the world, many homes can be found.
A cabin of logs,
Or a doghouse for dogs,
In the world, there are all kinds of homes!

Suggestions for Sharing

○ Have children use their hands and arms to suggest the details in each verse of the song. For example, they may put their fingertips together to form an igloo's dome. When children sing the chorus, have them make a circular, sweeping motion with their arms to suggest "homes all around."

○ Help children find pictures of the homes mentioned in the song. Have them each hold a picture to display at the appropriate time during the recital.

Thematic Activities

○ Let children use blocks, cardboard, clay, or other materials to build a model home. The model may be just one room or an entire dwelling. Later, let individuals display their work and describe the kinds of homes they've made. As an alternate activity, children may simply draw pictures of their homes.

○ Help children locate the places on a world map where igloos, adobes, tepees, houseboats, grass huts, yurts, hogans, and other types of homes can be found. Pin a small picture of each kind of home to its proper place on the map.

Classroom Resources

○ *Come to My Place* by Bobbie Kalman, Crabtree, 1985

○ *Have You Seen Houses?* by Joanne Oppenheim, Young Scott Books, 1973

○ *A House Is a House for Me* by Mary Ann Hoberman, Viking Press, 1978

WE ARE ONE WORLD

Pierre lives in Canada,
Maria lives in Spain.
But both like to ride their bikes
Along a shady lane.

Liv lives in Norway,
Ramon is in Peru.
But both laugh with the giraffe
When visiting the zoo.

Anwar is Egyptian,
Kim is Japanese.
But both run beneath the sun
And fly kites in the breeze.

Jack is from the U.S.A.
Karintha is from Chad.
But both write a poem at night
Upon a writing pad.

Children live all over,
The world's a giant ball.
But far or near, it's very clear
We're one world after all.

Suggestions for Sharing

○ Display a large world map on the classroom wall. Have children stand next to the map as they recite the poem and point to the places that are mentioned in each line.

○ Help children make flags of each country mentioned in the poem. Then, during recital, children can wave their flags as the appropriate countries are named.

Thematic Activities

○ As a class, research the countries mentioned in the poem as well as other countries of interest. Then work together to create a *We Are One World* big book. If you like, each child can write and illustrate a page.

○ Have children learn from older family members where their relatives may have lived before coming to this country. Pin an index card with the name of each child on the appropriate country on a large world map. Encourage volunteers to share interesting stories they have heard about relatives immigrating or adjusting to their new homes.

Classroom Resources

○ *How My Parents Learned to Eat* by Ina R. Friedman, Houghton Mifflin, 1984

○ *We Are All Alike...We Are All Different* by Cheltenham Elementary School Kindergartners, Scholastic, 1992

○ *Where in the World Do You Live?* by Al Hine and John Alcorn, Harcourt, 1962

THE DEEP BLUE SEA

Come along, come with me,
Take a dive in the deep blue sea.
Put on your gear, let's explore
All the way to the ocean floor!

See that snail wrapped in curls?
Look! An oyster wearing pearls!
Watch the octopus oh so dark,
But don't you dare to pet the shark!

CHORUS:
Dive on down, seaward bound,
Motion in the ocean is all around!
Dive on down, seaward bound,
Motion in the ocean is all around!

Now we're very far below,
The lantern fish are all aglow.
Is that a tiny shock you feel?
You just met an electric eel!

Giant blue whales start to stir,
Bigger than dinosaurs ever were!
Wave goodbye to the squid and sponge,
This is the end of our deep-sea plunge!

CHORUS

Suggestions for Sharing

○ Have children use their arms, hands, and fingers to imitate the movement of the ocean animals as they recite the poem. For example, they may curl their hands into a fist to imitate the snail or wriggle their fingers to imitate the octopus. During the chorus, they can point their arms straight ahead to indicate that they are diving.

○ Help children find pictures of the different sea animals mentioned in the poem. During the recital, have each child hold up one of the pictures at the appropriate time.

Thematic Activities

○ Have children imagine they discovered a new kind of fish or other sea creature in the ocean. Have them draw pictures of their discoveries. Then paste all pictures on a large sheet of blue oaktag to create a deep-sea collage.

○ Have children each choose a particular kind of ocean animal to learn more about. Then have them make information cards about their subjects. One side of the card should have a picture of the creature, the other side a list of several interesting facts about the creature. Use the cards to make a mobile to hang from the classroom ceiling.

Classroom Resources

○ *Creatures of the Sea* by John Christopher Fine, Atheneum, 1989

○ *Night Dive* by Ann McGovern, Macmillan, 1984

○ *Wonders of the Sea* by Louis Sabin, Troll, 1982

THE RAINFOREST

(sung to "Pussycat, Pussycat")

Rainforest, rainforest,
Covered with trees,
Home to the monkeys
And parrots and bees.
Rainforest, rainforest,
Who else is there?
Butterflies, toucans,
And bats in the air.

Rainforest, rainforest,
Covered with green,
Flowers and ferns
Like the world's never seen.
Rainforest, rainforest,
What's on the ground?
Lizards and pythons
Are creeping around.

Rainforest, rainforest,
Covered with rain,
Growing the plants
That we hope will remain.
Rainforest, rainforest,
Why do we care?
To make sure the rainforest
Always is there.

Suggestions for Sharing

○ Have children use their hands and fingers to imitate the movements of the rainforest creatures moving about. For example, fluttering hands can represent butterflies and bats, while creeping fingers can represent pythons and lizards.

○ Help children decide on different rhythm instruments that can be used to represent the various rainforest animals and rain in the song. For example, a triangle might represent the butterfly, and sandblocks could represent pythons and lizards. After students decide on their roles, they should begin playing their instruments when their animals or the rain is mentioned in the song and keep playing until the song's end.

Thematic Activities

○ Have children make their own model rainforest in the classroom. Using a large cardboard box or glass tank as the base, have them put in grass, leaves, twigs, bugs, and other examples of plants and animal life. Have groups of children create special habitats for the animals who might live in their rainforest.

○ Talk about the current debate over whether or not rainforest trees should be cut down. Explain both sides of the issue (developers' needs versus the preservation of rare plants and animals), and let children express their opinions. Have them write a local or national environmental organization for more information on the topic.

Classroom Resources

○ *The Great Kapok Tree: A Tale of the Amazon Rain Forest* by Lynne Cherry, Harcourt, Brace, Jovanovich, 1991

○ *Rain Forest* by Helen Cowcher, Farrar, Straus, & Giroux, 1988

○ *Where the Forest Meets the Sea* by Jeannie Baker, Greenwillow, 1987

THE SOLAR SYSTEM

(sung to "Twinkle, Twinkle, Little Star")

Twinkle, twinkle, little star,
Oh so bright and oh so far.
In the sky, a tiny dot,
Glowing gas that's very hot!
Twinkle, twinkle, little star,
Oh so bright and oh so far.

Beaming, beaming, gleaming moon,
Like a giant white balloon.
Round and round the Earth you spin,
Through the month, new shapes you're in.
Beaming, beaming, gleaming moon,
Like a giant white balloon.

Glowing, glowing, red-hot sun,
Shining light on everyone.
Earth goes round you once a year,
You're a star with atmosphere!
Glowing, glowing, red-hot sun,
Shining light on everyone.

Suggestions for Sharing

○ Divide the class into three groups: stars, moons, and suns. Have children make cardboard representations of their heavenly bodies to wear as they perform the song.

○ Have all the stars form a large circle, with the moons and suns standing inside. During the first verse, have the stars wave their arms to indicate twinkling. During the second verse, have the moons walk around the inside of the circle to represent orbiting. During the third verse, have the suns spin slowly to represent rotation.

Thematic Activities

○ Make a class mobile of the solar system. Children may use items such as tinfoil balls, yellow tennis balls, and white whiffle balls to represent the stars, sun, moon, and planets. Hang each item from string tied to the ceiling to create a giant solar system.

○ Use resources (e.g., *The Farmer's Almanac,* an encyclopedia, children's nonfiction books such as *The Moon Seems to Change* by Franklyn M. Branley, Harper Trophy Books, 1987) to help children understand about the different phases of the moon. Then encourage children to look for the moon every night for a month in order to draw its changing configurations. (Hint: Try offering children copies of reproducible blank calendar pages so they may easily record their moon observations.)

Classroom Resources

○ *The Magic School Bus Lost in the Solar System* by Joanna Cole, Scholastic, 1990

○ *The Planets in Our Solar System* by Franklyn M. Branley, Crowell, 1981

○ *Stargazers* by Gail Gibbons, Holiday House, 1992

MACHINES

(sung to "The Wheels on the Bus")

The wheels on machines go round and round,
Round and round, round and round.
The wheels on machines go round and round,
Whirring their sound.

The pins on machines go ping, ping, ping,
Ping, ping, ping, ping, ping, ping.
The pins on machines go ping, ping, ping,
Pulling the spring.

The rods on machines go side to side,
Side to side, side to side.
The rods on machines go side to side,
See how they slide.

The pulleys on machines go up and down,
Up and down, up and down.
The pulleys on machines go up and down,
High off the ground.

The screws on machines go twist, twist, twist,
Twist, twist, twist, twist, twist, twist.
The screws on machines go twist, twist, twist,
Twist like your wrist!

Suggestions for Sharing

○ Have children use their arms, hands, and fingers to simulate the different movements of the machine parts. For example, their hands can circle "round and round," their fingers can point "ping, ping, ping," and their arms can slide "side to side."

○ Assign a different machine part to each child or group of children. Have them all stand side by side. After each child or group has sung its individual verse, let the entire class sing all the verses simultaneously, to give the impression of all the machine parts working together.

Thematic Activities

○ Have children talk about the different machines they use each day, such as alarm clocks, radios, refrigerators, and cars. Let each child draw a picture of a particular kind of machine they rely on. Use the pictures to create a collage entitled "Machines We Depend Upon."

○ Encourage each child to invent a new kind of machine, such as a bed maker-upper or a homework solver. Children may draw pictures of their inventions or make actual models. Let them display their inventions and describe what they do and how they work.

Classroom Resources

○ *Biggest Machines* by Denise Kiley, Raintree, 1980

○ *Big Work Machines* by Patricia Relf, Golden 1984

○ *The Laziest Robot in Zone One* by Lillian and Phoebe Hoban, HarperCollins, 1983

TRAVELING, TRAVELING

(sung to "Row, Row, Row Your Boat")

Row, row, row your boat,
Gently round the lake.
Traveling, traveling on the water,
Boats are what you take.

Drive, drive, drive your car,
Have a merry cruise.
Traveling, traveling on the road,
Cars are what you use.

Fly, fly, fly your plane,
High up in the air.
Traveling, traveling through the sky,
Planes will get you there.

Chug, chug, chug your train,
Chug along the track.
Traveling, traveling on the rails,
Trains go there and back.

Stamp, stamp, stamp your feet,
Stamp them on the ground.
Traveling, traveling on your feet,
Walk to get around!

Suggestions for Sharing

○ Divide the class into five groups and assign each a different verse of the song. Have each group sing its verse aloud while performing its actions (rowing a boat, driving a car, etc.).

○ After all verses have been sung, have the groups sing the entire song again in a round, each joining in one line after the previous group has begun. Invite all children to parade around the classroom while acting out their individual modes of travel.

Thematic Activities

○ Have each child use papier-mache, clay, cardboard, or other materials to build a model transportation machine, such as a sports car, a jet plane, or a submarine. Invite children to display their models and describe how they made them.

○ Organize children into three groups. Have each group find magazine pictures to create a collage of transportation used on the ground, in the air, or on water. For example, the air collage might include airplanes, blimps, helicopters, rockets, and parachutes. Display all three collages on the bulletin board.

Classroom Resources

○ *How Do We Travel?* by Caroline Arnold, Watts, 1983

○ *On the Go* by Ann Morris, Lothrop, Lee, & Shepard, 1990

○ *This Is the Way We Go to School* by Edith Baer, Scholastic, 1990

THE HARE AND
THE TORTOISE

Did you hear about the race between Tortoise and Hare?
Go, go, go! Go, go, go!
No one thought it would be fair,
No, no, no! No, no, no!
Hare was fast with legs so strong,
Go, go, go! Go, go, go!
Tortoise only crept along,
Slow, slow, slow! Slow, slow, slow!

Round the lake they went to race,
Go, go, go! Go, go, go!
Each one at a different pace,
Oh, oh, oh! Oh, oh, oh!
Hare was so sure he was best,
Go, go, go! Go, go, go!
He ran ahead, then stopped to rest,
Whoa, whoa, whoa! Whoa, whoa, whoa!

Meanwhile Tortoise slowly crept,
Slow, slow, slow! Slow, slow, slow!
Passing Hare who soundly slept,
Oh, oh, oh! Oh, oh, oh!
Guess which runner took first place?
Go, go, go! Go, go, go!
Slow and steady wins the race,
Ho, ho, ho! Ho, ho, ho!

Suggestions for Sharing

○ Have children stand in place and stamp their feet on each word of the refrains "Go, go, go," "No, no, no," and so on. Or have them march around the classroom as they recite, taking a small step on each word of the refrains.

○ Have children use their hands to represent the tortoise and the hare. Every time one of the animals moves, children can wiggle their fingers upside down to indicate traveling.

Thematic Activities

○ Help children learn more about the differences between hares and tortoises. Create an information chart that compares their sizes, weights, body features, speeds, homes, and eating habits. If you wish, add more animals to the chart. Help children to determine which animals can travel the fastest.

○ Have children participate in running races. Provide timekeepers with stopwatches to time each run. See who the fastest runners in class are. Contests might also include wheelbarrow races and three-legged races.

Classroom Resources

○ *The Hare and the Tortoise* by Aesop, Troll, 1981

○ *The Hare and the Tortoise* by Brian Wildsmith, Watts, 1966

○ *I Wish I Could Fly* by Ron Maris, Greenwillow, 1986

SAFETY FIRST!

(sung to "Skip to My Lou")

CHORUS:
Rules, rules, stick to the rules,
Rules, rules, stick to the rules,
Rules, rules, stick to the rules,
Stick to the rules for safety!

Look both ways when crossing the street,
Cars must make a stop complete,
Use your eyes before your feet,
Stick to the rules for safety!

CHORUS

Don't light matches, it's no game,
Things can quickly catch aflame,
Fire spreads, and that's a shame,
Stick to the rules for safety!

CHORUS

Never run by a swimming pool,
You could slip and be a fool,
Walk instead and play it cool,
Stick to the rules for safety!

CHORUS

Don't throw rocks that you have found,
You might hit someone around,
Leave them safely on the ground,
Stick to the rules for safety!

CHORUS

Suggestions for Sharing

○ Have children imitate the actions in each verse of the song, emphasizing the right ways to behave. For example, they may pretend to be looking both ways before crossing, putting down a book of matches, walking by a pool, and leaving rocks on the ground.

○ Each time the chorus is sung, have children wag their index finger as if giving a warning about sticking to the rules.

Thematic Activities

○ Talk about important safety rules to observe. Then have children work individually or with partners to create large oaktag posters advertising critical rules of safety, such as "Look Both Ways Before Crossing." Encourage children to illustrate their posters. Display all work prominently in the classroom.

○ Invite guest speakers to your class, such as a firefighter, a lifeguard, and a crossing guard. Have them discuss the importance of safety rules. Encourage children to prepare questions to ask each guest during the visit.

Classroom Resources

○ *At Home* by Pete Sanders, Gloucester Press, 1989

○ *Blue Bug's Safety Book* by Virginia Poulet, Childrens Press, 1973

○ *What Should You Do When—?* by Amy Bahr, Grosset & Dunlap, 1986

WORKING ON TRASH!

(sung to "I've Been Working on the Railroad")

We've been working on **recycling**
All the trash we can.
We've been working on recycling,
It's a very simple plan.
Separate your glass and paper,
Separate your plastic and tin.
Take the trash that you've recycled
To your recycling bin!

We've been working on **reducing**
All the trash we can.
We've been working on reducing,
It's a very simple plan.
Don't go wasting any products,
Use just exactly what you need.
Don't buy things in extra wrapping,
Reduce and you'll succeed!

We've been working on **reusing**
All the trash we can.
We've been working on reusing,
It's a very simple plan.
If it's a paper bag you're using,
Don't use it once, use it twice!
Give old clothes and toys to someone,
To reuse them would be nice!

Suggestions for Sharing

○ Divide the class into three groups. Have each group perform a different verse of the song. Children in each group can wear signs that say either Recycling, Reducing, or Reusing.

○ Have children recycle paper bags into song vests that they may wear while singing this (and other) song(s). For each vest you will need to cut a straight line down the middle of the large side of a brown grocery bag, starting at the top edge and cutting to the bottom. At the bottom, make a circular cut large enough to fit the child's neck comfortably. Invert the bag and place the paper bag vest on a child. On each vest, mark a spot to cut armholes. After armholes have been cut, children may use crayons to decorate the vests (one symbol for each song learned, perhaps!). Children may also "fringe" vests by making snips along the bottom edges.

Thematic Activities

○ Talk with children about the current problems we face with our trash, including a shortage of disposal sites and the pollution of our land, water, and air. Ask children to suggest possible ways we can cut down on our trash problems. Then have them design posters that advertise the solutions they came up with.

○ Have the class keep track of all the paper, plastic, and other trash it creates in a school week. Have children separate materials in large plastic bags and weigh them each day to determine how much trash they have made. See if the class can "lose weight" during the following week.

Classroom Resources

○ *About Garbage and Stuff* by Ann Zane Shanks, Viking Press, 1973

○ *Just a Dream* by Chris Van Allsburg, Houghton, 1990

○ *Recycle It, Once Is Not Enough* by Stuart Kallen, Rockbottom Books, 1990

BUILDING A SNOWMAN

Roll a snowball on the ground,
Roll it till it's big and round,
Pack the snow—pound, pound, pound!
That's the bottom of your snowman!

Roll a second ball of snow,
Roll and roll and watch it grow,
Plop it on the ball below,
That's the middle of your snowman!

Start to roll just one more ball,
Make it round but slightly small,
Place on top—don't let it fall!
That's the top of your snowman!

Use a button for each eye,
A carrot nose you then apply,
Place a hat on way up high,
You've got yourself a snowman!

Suggestions for Sharing

○ Let children imitate the actions in the poem by having them "roll" their hands as if making a snowball. Also have them "pound" the snow and then lift it with their arms.

○ You may wish to organize the children into four groups. As they recite, have one group make the first snowball, another group make the second, another make the third, and the last group add the items to the head.

Thematic Activities

○ Offer children white or beige clay dough and invite them to roll the clay into balls and skewer the balls onto toothpicks to create clay snowpeople. Snowpeople may be decorated with scraps of fabric or paper, bits of plastic (toothpaste-tube caps make great snowpeople hats) or foil, or twigs. Snowpeople may then be placed together on a large mirror resting flat on a table or desktop. Twigs pressed into additional balls of clay can serve as wintertime trees, and a sprinkling of soapflakes or wisps of cotton may be added to complete the wintery display.

○ Talk about how snow feels when it is used to make a snowman. Have children compare snow to other building materials such as mud, clay, sand, and brick. How are they alike? How are they different? Create a comparison chart that lists the similarities and differences between snow and other materials.

Classroom Resources

○ *Building the Snowman* by Raymond Briggs, Little Brown, 1985

○ *The Snowy Day* by Ezra Jack Keats, Viking Press, 1963

○ *A Winter Day* by Douglas Florian, Greenwillow, 1987

WHAT TO WEAR?

What to wear? What to wear?
It all depends on the weather.
Look outside, then decide.
Here, let's do it together.

Pitter-patter! Pitter-patter!
See the rainy sky.
Wear your raincoat and your boots
To keep you nice and dry!

Hooray, hooray! A sunny day!
Let's play by the pool.
Wear a lightweight shirt and shorts
So you'll be nice and cool.

Yo ho! Yo ho! A blanket of snow!
Last night there was a storm.
Wear a coat, a scarf, and gloves
And boots to keep you warm!

Whoosh! Whoosh! Poor little bush!
The wind is making it sway.
Wear a sweater when you go out
So you don't catch cold today!

Suggestions for Sharing

○ Organize children into four groups and have each group dress to match one of the verses of the poem (excluding the first verse). One group may dress in raincoats and boots, another group in light-weight shirts and shorts, and so on.

○ Have all children recite the first verse together. Then have each group step forward when reciting its own verse. Children may perform actions such as holding umbrellas, fanning themselves in the sun, shivering in the snow, or walking against a strong wind.

Thematic Activities

○ Talk about the different kinds of weather that children experience throughout the year. Divide the class into groups and have each group prepare a collage of magazine pictures showing people dressed for snowy weather, rainy weather, windy weather, and hot weather.

○ Talk about the different kinds of materials that clothing is made of, such as cotton, corduroy, wool, leather, and silk. Display samples of each kind of material. Have children feel each piece and tell whether it is heavy or light. See if children can identify the material of the clothing they are wearing.

Classroom Resources

○ *Caps, Hats, Socks, and Mittens* by Louise Borden, Scholastic, 1989

○ *The Jacket I Wear in the Snow* by Shirley Neitzel, Greenwillow, 1989

○ *What Will the Weather Be Like Today?* by Paul Rogers, Greenwillow, 1990

BOOKS ARE GREAT!

CHORUS:
Books are great! Books are fun!
Books let you do what you've never done!
Books are cool! Books are in!
Books let you go where you've never been!

Read a good mystery, solve a crime!
Read about history, go back in time!
Read about outer space, land on Mars!
Read about an auto race, zoom with the cars!

CHORUS

Read about a haunted house, shake to your knees!
Read about a cat and mouse, run for the cheese!
Read about a lost dog, where can it be?
Read about a giant frog under the sea!

CHORUS

Read a very funny book, blues go away!
Read a bright, sunny book on a rainy day!
Read a goodnight book, just before bed,
Let a sleep-tight book dance in your head!

CHORUS

Suggestions for Sharing

○ Have children recite the chorus together, but assign individual lines for the verses. Give each child a book to hold. As each line of the poem is recited, have children turn a page of their books, as if they are reading them.

○ Let children dress in costumes to represent the possible characters in their books. For example, the child reciting the line about mysteries might dress in a detective's hat. Encourage children to perform the actions that the characters in their books might do, such as looking through a detective's magnifying glass.

Thematic Activities

○ Take a survey to learn what kinds of books children like to read most (mysteries, adventure stories, comedies, etc.). Display the results in a bar graph or a chart. Encourage volunteers to describe favorite books they've read.

○ Have the class visit your school library, where the librarian can show where different types of books are located. Older children should learn how to use the card catalog or computer to locate books by their titles, authors, or subject matter. Have each child choose one book to read and report on later. Keep a large chart that tallies how many books the class has read throughout the year.

Classroom Resources

○ *How a Book Is Made* by Aliki, Crowell, 1986

○ *Let's Go to the Library* by Lisl Weil, Holiday House, 1990

○ *Reading Is Fun with Bobby Bookworm* by Greg Hildebrandt, Unicorn, 1988

SHARING, CARING FRIENDS

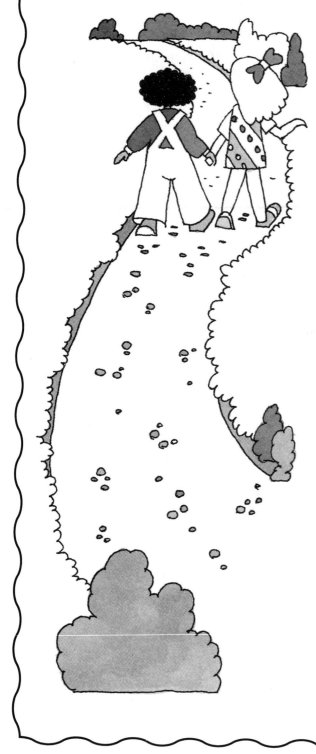

(sung to "Camptown Races")

What is fun for friends to do?
Sharing! Caring!
Who am I and who are you?
Sharing, caring friends!
I like you, and you like me,
Sharing! Caring!
It's the nicest thing to be,
Sharing, caring friends!

CHORUS:
Being a friend all day,
Being a friend all night.
Whether times are glad or sad,
Friends will make them right!

Share your dog, I'll share my cat,
Sharing! Caring!
Share your ball, I'll share my bat,
Sharing, caring friends!
Share your peach, I'll share my plum,
Sharing! Caring!
Share your horn, I'll share my drum,
Sharing, caring friends!

CHORUS

Suggestions for Sharing

○ Have each child pair off with a partner. Every time the words *sharing* and *caring* are mentioned in the song, have the partners either shake hands or hug one another.

○ Have children gather the items mentioned in the second verse of the song. (A stuffed toy dog and cat may be used instead of real ones!) As the items are mentioned during the recital, have partners trade the items with one another.

Thematic Activities

○ Write all the children's names on individual slips of paper. Place them in a bowl and have each child draw a slip. Have the children think of something nice to say about the classmate whose name they have drawn (for example, "Mike is a good speller."). Record their statements on a Friendship Chart and hang it on the wall.

○ Ask each child to bring something to class to share with everyone. It might be a favorite toy, a small pet, or a pretty picture, for example. Let everyone have a chance to enjoy the item.

Classroom Resources

○ *Do You Want to Be My Friend?* by Eric Carle, Crowell, 1971

○ *What Mary Jo Shared* by Janice May Udry, Whitman, 1966

○ *Will I Have a Friend?* by Miriam Cohen, Macmillan, 1967

SOMEONE'S BIRTHDAY

(sung to "London Bridge Is Falling Down")

Someone's birthday is today,
Is today, is today.
Someone's birthday is today,
And it's (name)!

Let's prepare a birthday cake,
Birthday cake, birthday cake.
Let's prepare a birthday cake,
Just for (name)!

Add a candle for each year,
For each year, for each year.
Add a candle for each year,
Just for (name)!

Make a special birthday card,
Birthday card, birthday card.
Make a special birthday card,
Just for (name)!

Sing a happy birthday song,
Birthday song, birthday song.
Sing a happy birthday song,
Just for (name)!

Suggestions for Sharing

○ Have children stand in a circle with the birthday person in the middle. As they sing, children walk around the circle, pointing to the person each time his or her name is mentioned.

○ Have children act out the actions in the song (baking a cake, putting on candles, and designing a card). On the final verse, children may clap their hands together in rhythm.

Thematic Activities

○ Ask each child to draw a self-portrait and to write his or her birth date (month and day only) under the picture. String all pictures in chronological order along the wall to serve as a birthday time line to refer to throughout the year.

○ Provide each child with a piece of construction paper folded in half to resemble a birthday card. On the front of each card have students print "Happy Birthday to_____," leaving space to later add a student's name. Students may then use crayons, markers, stickers and glued-on glitter to decorate the outside of the card. Collect the cards and store in a box with scissors, glue, and a selection of toy and book catalogs. On a student's birthday, pull a card from the box and fill in the birthday child's name. Have students look through catalogs and cut out pictures of gifts they wish they could give the birthday child. Have students glue pictures collage-style on the inside of the card, which will be presented to the birthday child at the end of the day.

Classroom Resources

○ *Clifford's Birthday Party* by Norman Bridwell, Scholastic, 1988

○ *Happy Birthday, Ronald Morgan!* by Patricia Reilly Giff, Viking, 1986

○ *Some Birthday!* by Patricia Polacco, Simon and Schuster, 1991

FAMILIES ARE
ALL DIFFERENT!

(sung to "Ten Little Indians")

Are there two or three or four
In a family?
Five or six or more
In a family?
I'm in a family,
You're in a family,
Families are all different!

Some have fathers,
Some have mothers,
Some have sisters,
Some have brothers,
Some have cousins,
Some have others,
Families are all different!

Families large,
And families small,
And families short,
And families tall.
They're not the same,
As you'll recall,
Families are all different!

Suggestions for Sharing

○ In the first verse, have children hold up fingers to indicate the numbers they are singing about (two, three, four, five, and six). Also, have them point to themselves and then to a classmate to indicate "I'm in a family, you're in a family."

○ In the second and third verses, children can pop up one finger at a time when listing different family members and types of families. On the line "Families are all different," children can wiggle all ten fingers.

Thematic Activities

○ Invite children to draw pictures or bring in photos of their families. Let them take turns describing one or more of their family members. Place all pictures on a large bulletin board display titled "Families Are All Different."

○ Have children draw pictures showing favorite activities they like to do with their families. Also have each child write or dictate a sentence to go with the picture. Display all work on the classroom wall.

Classroom Resources

○ *Families Are Different* by Nina Pellegrini, Holiday House, 1991

○ *Family* by Helen Oxenbury, Simon & Schuster, 1981

○ *On Mother's Lap* by Ann Herbert Scott, Clarion, 1992

MY FEELINGS

There are things I have that I can't see,
Things that change inside of me.
What, oh what, can those things be?
My feelings!

When a friend calls up and says, "Let's play,"
When I work in school and get an "A,"
When my favorite dinner's on its way,
I'm **happy**!

When I can't go out because of rain,
When my tummy hurts and I'm in pain,
When my favorite toy goes down the drain,
I'm **sad**!

When thunder booms, and the lights go out,
When suddenly I hear a shout,
When an ugly bug will crawl about,
I'm **afraid**!

At times I'm happy, at times I'm sad,
At times I'm scared, at times I'm glad.
I know I'm me, because I've had
My feelings!

Suggestions for Sharing

○ Read the poem one line at a time and have children decide together on motions to help turn the poem into a fingerplay.

○ Put special emphasis on the feeling named at the end of each verse. For happy, children may throw out their arms in joy. For sad, they may rub their eyes as if crying. For afraid, they may cover their face with their hands.

Thematic Activities

○ Invite children to talk about the things that make them happy, sad, or afraid. Also discuss other emotions they may experience, such as being angry, surprised, or confused. Stress the idea that it is all right to have different feelings at different times.

○ Have students brainstorm a list of things that might make them feel happy, sad, afraid, upset, worried, tired, etc. On a large chart pad, just list the stimuli (eating, climbing, singing, shopping, playing ball, taking a bath, etc.) without the feeling responses (as these may vary from child to child). Then provide students with large pieces of manila paper which have been preprinted with the sentence: *When I _____, I feel_____*. Have students refer to the list for inspiration. Then help students fill in the blanks on their papers and have them draw pictures to go with their writing. After students have had a chance to share their individual ideas and pictures, collect them into a book entitled "We Feel Lots of Different Feelings."

Classroom Resources

○ *Alexander and the Terrible, Horrible, No Good, Very Bad Day* by Judith Viorst, Atheneum, 1972

○ *Feelings* by Aliki, Greenwillow, 1984

○ *The Way I Feel Sometimes* by Beatrice Schenk de Regniers, Clarion, 1988

WHAT WILL YOU BE?

Doctor, dancer, office clerk,
What's your favorite kind of work?
Miner, designer, baking cake,
What's the job that you will take?

Barber, farmer, animal vet,
What position will you get?
Tailor, sailor, engineer,
What'll you pick for your career?

Work with people,
Work alone,
Work all day on the telephone.
Work in an office,
Work outdoors,
Where will you work?
The choice is yours!

Driver, diver, fighting fires,
What's the job of your desires?
Teacher, painter, selling shoes,
What's the job that you will choose?

Suggestions for Sharing

○ Assign each child a role in the poem (doctor, dancer, etc.). Encourage children to dress as their characters, and then line them up. During the recital, as each character is mentioned, have the child playing that part step forward or raise his or her hand.

○ Instead of children dressing in costume, have them draw pictures of their characters. As the poem is recited, each child holds up his or her picture when the character is mentioned.

Thematic Activities

○ Hold a Career Day in class. Invite parents and other friends to speak to the class about their jobs. Have them describe their daily routines, the training that is necessary for their position, and other relevant information. Encourage children to ask their guests questions during or after each presentation.

○ Have the children each choose a career they would like to have. Give everyone a turn to tell classmates why they chose that job and to describe the kind of work it involves.

Classroom Resources

○ *Jeremy's Decision* by Ardyth Brott, Kane/Miller, 1990

○ *Mommies at Work* by Eve Merriam, Simon and Schuster, 1989

○ *Muppets in My Neighborhood* by Harry McNaught, Random House, 1977

I'M ME!

In the mirror
What do I see?
Someone special,
That is me!

My eyes, my ears,
My lips, my nose.
No one's looks are
Just like those!

All my favorite
Things to do
Are not all
The same for you.

What I like
To eat and drink,
What I like
To say and think.

How I laugh,
How I talk,
How I run,
How I walk.

In the mirror
What do I see?
Someone special,
That is me!

Suggestions for Sharing

○ Have children hold mirrors as they recite the poem. In the second verse, let them point to each facial feature that is mentioned. Also, have them imitate motions such as eating, drinking, talking, and laughing.

○ Assign each child a partner. Have the partners face each other as they recite the poem together. Partners may perform identical hand gestures (pointing to their facial features, etc.) as they recite.

Thematic Activities

○ Ask children to bring in baby pictures of themselves. Display all the pictures on the bulletin board. See if the class can identify each one correctly. Let classmates point out the specific features in each photo that aided them in their identification.

○ Have each child create a book entitled "I'm Me!" On each page of the book, the child should write a sentence such as *My favorite game is* _____. Have them draw pictures to go with the sentences. When all pages are completed, staple them together to make a personalized book.

Classroom Resources

○ *I Like Me* by Nancy Carlson, Viking Penguin, 1988

○ *Is This You?* by Ruth Krauss and Crockett Johnson, Scholastic, 1988

○ *Just Me* by Marie Hall Ets, Viking, 1988